I0426609

The No-Nonsense Guide to Flood Safety (2nd Edition)

Jeffery D. Sims

Books may be purchased by contacting the publisher and author at Lulu.com, Amazon.com, or contact the author at:

Beyond The Spectrum Books
http://beyond-the-political-spectrum.blogspot.com/

Cover Design: Jeffery D. Sims
Publisher: Lulu Books & Beyond The Spectrum Books
ISBN 978-1-304-70945-590000
1. Reference 2. Science 3. Weather 4. Safety 5. Floods
Second Edition
Printed in North Carolina, USA

Acknowledgement

For Maxine, Donnie, & Aaron (good friends who I'm hoping are as surprised to have actually witnessed this happening).

Table of Contents

Introduction

   Simply put, in some ways I was a normal child while in other ways, I was anything but. It is the abnormal part of my being which accounts for why you are holding this book in your hot little hands (or reading it on your tablet). While I enjoyed watching cartoons, reading comic books, and favored science-fiction (notice a pattern?), I was also fascinated—infatuated actually—with learning about strange, unusual, and otherwise unexplained uncommon events. Whether the subject was verifying the legitimacy of alleged occurrences explored in the field of parapsychology, learning about what things exist beyond the boundaries of our planet through the area of astronomy, or—of relevance to you the reader—understanding the causes of interesting weather phenomenon like tornadoes and hurricanes.

   As an adult, my love of learning had grown to encompass many other subjects, including history and politics (which I went to college to study). I had come to the awareness that I had/have an innate thirst for knowledge, about everything around me. As a result, I have more books than I will ever read, probably more than the average person. I've also probably had more different types of jobs than the average person. I've done a great deal of living. And in everything I've read, done, and observed, I've taken a great deal of awareness about life and the nature of the universe around us with me (yes, I know...a little grandiose, if not self-centered-sounding). I suppose by way of osmosis, I had also developed a love of teaching after having fallen into the vocation of substitute and adult education instructor. Because of these experiences, I have been driven to observe the world with an attempt to gain a deeper meaning of it all...and maybe bring a little bit of insight to others.

   I am also driven to write about my observations –without the latent bias of emotion, beliefs, or cultural beliefs—in order to convey a semblance of truth (the "teacher" in me I suppose) and maybe give others a little something to think about. This is why I started blogging and writing regularly some years ago. In an indirect way, writing is also a way for me to help others to think about and offer possible solutions to grander problems posed by counterproductive policies and our own individual thinking. But it was only recently that I was motivated to combine my proclivity for (objective) observation, thirst for learning, and ultimately my writing to create a series of books based on my own intellectual curiosities and love for seeking solutions to existing problems.

   This resulting compendium of interests and ideas has the (intended) benefit of imparting in those who chose to purchase and read it a level of awareness and knowledge about the an aspect of the dangers –those presented by the earth we live on—inherent in the world around us. And although there are no certain safe places to hide from real-life dangers, there *are* places as well as courses of actions that one can take to limit exposure to these dangers. I acknowledge this fact throughout the book(s) by using terms like *relatively*, *comparatively*, or variations of such words to convey that the suggestions offered are in, all likelihood based on research and other findings, the best options given the dangers and circumstances.

   It is my hope that the information in this book (or as I call it, "safety manual") will save a life, or at least prevent serious injury to those who would might be affected by a related dangerous experience.

   So without further ado, I present to you, the revised edition of The No-Nonsense Guide to Flood Safety...
--Jeffery D. Sims

Floods

What Are They?

Floods are among the most common disruptive weather-related occurrence in the world. A flood is a short-term overflow of water that covers and submerges areas of land that are normally dry. What makes floods so dangerous is that, outside of heat waves, more people are killed by them each year than any other type of weather-related disaster—including tornadoes, hurricanes, and blizzards. Depending on the type, length, and duration of a particular flood, floodwaters often damage property to the tune of hundreds of millions of dollars each year, as well as create multiple potential health and environmental risks for those affected—this in addition to the obvious drowning hazard. Because of this, floods are particularly dangerous to both people and property.

The photo above illustrates the extent of flooding in the city of New Orleans, Louisiana in the aftermath of 2005's Hurricane Katrina. One of many failures in the city's flood control system during the storm, this particular flooding is the result of the failure of the 17th Street Canal levee, which is directly linked to adjacent Lake Pontchartrain.

How Do They Form?

On the whole, there are three primary factors that make up the textbook definition of a flood: the amount of excess water, the period of time it takes for [the] excess the water to fill a particular area, and the size of the area [the] water has to fill. Floods generally form as a result of water, in excess of the expected or normal amounts, arriving into an area of normally dry land. Floods tend to occur on flat and/or in low-lying areas, when the ground is oversaturated with water which is unable to either run-off or cannot run-off quickly enough to stop accumulating.

Although many *overland floods* (the slow-paced, most common type of flooding) occur over a given period of time such as days or even weeks, *flash floods*—defined as a rapid submerging of land by quickly rising and/or moving water occurring within 6 hours of a precipitating event—can result in raging waters in as little as a few minutes. *Flash floods* are the most dangerous type of flood because of how quickly, and sometimes forcefully their waters can inundate an area. Flash floods often form with little or no previous warning. Because of this fact, most deaths from floods result from flash floods. Flash floods can contain rocks, mud, or other debris that is often carried away by the sweeping tide of their waters. Floods of either type are often the result of other types of natural or man-made hazards. The most notable causes of floods include:

- Thunderstorms/Heavy Rains – Localized heavy rains from slow-moving storms (or a prolonged series of storms) over the same area can cause flooding over time, if the rainfall exceeds the ability of the natural (and manmade) drainage systems to compensate. This means that streams, rivers, and drainage systems can be overwhelmed by the abundance water to the point where the water has nowhere to runoff, accumulating and rising on the ground. The likelihood of flooding is increased if the ground is already saturated with an abundance of moisture. Furthermore, flash flooding can occur when small creeks and streams overflow their banks during heavy rainfalls to the point where surrounding areas begin experience fast-rising waters—especially on uneven and/or hilly terrains.

- Hurricanes/Tropical Storms/Monsoons – Tropical weather systems such as hurricanes and tropical storms, that typically affect coastal areas, contain two inherent components that nearly guarantee that flooding will occur in their wake—high winds, and torrential rains. These twin dangers invariably create *storm surges* (a rise in water from an offshore source such as an ocean, which is primarily driven by high winds) along or near coastal areas, which can also cause flooding many miles/kilometers inland. Additionally, the rainfall and subsequent flooding generated by these storms that can be especially damaging since the rain collects in localized areas. While all coastal areas are at risk, certain areas are particularly vulnerable to flooding. The best example of an especially destructive flood occurring in particularly high-risk areas was 2005's Hurricane Katrina, which devastated large swaths in the city of New Orleans, Louisiana and the coastal regions of Mississippi. Both of these low-lying areas in relation to their proximity to large bodies of water made them especially susceptible to the floods and storm surges generated by the storm.

Monsoons, seasonal changes in weather patterns that typically result in steady heavy rains, are somewhat predictable weather episodes that can result in both overland as well as flash floods over the affected areas. In the United States, monsoons generally affect areas of the country's desert Southwest. The result of these heavy-rain episodes quite often is the rapid filling of natural and manmade *gullies* and/or *washes* with moving streams of water that can easily overflow the boundaries of these water channels.

- Post-Winter Thawing - During early spring, still-frozen land often prevents melting snow or rainfall from seeping into the ground. The water from thawing snow then runs off the hardened surface of the relatively cold ground and flows into nearby lakes, streams, and rivers. Any overflow of water to these waterways will cause them to spill over their banks and flood nearby lands. Add seasonal storms to the process, and the result is often severe spring flooding.
- Levee/Dikes/Dam Breaches - Levees (interchangeably called *dikes* in other regions, especially in Northern Europe) are manmade and/or natural barriers structured along the course of waterways, and designed to protect potentially flood-prone areas nearby from rising waters.[1] However, levees can—although rarely—do fail at times as a result of intense weather events (such as a strong hurricane), causing them to be overtopped or breached by rising water. The result is the increased probability of flooding.
- Other Destructive Occurrences – Other naturally-occurring phenomena such as earthquakes, volcanic eruptions, and mudslides can trigger floods by way impacting waterways near the areas of their occurrences. Large amounts of debris or rapidly-shifting geological patterns can often result in flash-flooding of both uninhabited land as well as population centers near where these events happen.
- Construction/Development - Construction and development can change the natural drainage patterns of a given region can create brand new flood risks. That's because new buildings, parking lots, and roads mean less land to absorb excess precipitation from heavy rains and tropical storms. Furthermore, manmade accidents that may or may not be related to construction can result in flooding, such as that which occurred underneath the city of Chicago, Illinois in 1992. In that particular incident, on-going construction above a long-abandoned tunnel underneath the nearby Chicago River resulted in a leak. That leak allowed water from the river to eventually flood a large portion of the city's downtown's business district below ground, causing nearly $2 billion (US) dollars in damage to the affected area's infrastructure.

On the whole, floods can potentially occur anyplace water can gather in abundance. Depending on the circumstances, floods can affect an area a small as a few feet/meters, to several hundred miles/kilometers. They can be the result of shifting weather patterns over a period of duration, or they can be the result of a single rapid-paced event. A given geographical area may receive its usual annual rainfall over the course of a year without any discernible issues. However, if this same amount of rainfall occurs over a considerable shorter period such over several days, flooding is likely to be the result.

---

[1] The terms dike and levee have been used interchangeably to describe certain water barriers. Historically, a *dike* is used to divert or restrain flood water from tidal bodies of water such as oceans and/or seas. A *levee*, on the other hand, diverts or restrains flood waters from streams, rivers, and/or lakes, such as the system of levees which protect cities along the Mississippi River

Areas with greater absorbency, like forests and fields can handle more rain. But in developed areas, which are usually covered in asphalt or concrete, the ground can't absorb much water. In these populated areas, a flood's danger is naturally magnified, potentially resulting in a great deal of property damage, economic costs, and loss of human life. And even after flood waters *recede* (the process of flood waters drying up and/or withdrawing back into the normal boundaries of nearby waterways), there are lingering dangers which are potentially as detrimental to both life and property as the flood waters themselves. For this reason, it is important to understand the dangers associated with flood waters and how to limit their impact on those floods might adversely affect.

The damage illustrated in the photo is an example of damage flash flooding can inflict on a regions infrastructure.

What Makes Them Dangerous?

Floods adversely affect the lives of so many people, resulting in an <u>average</u> of 100 deaths a year in the U.S., and many more worldwide. Floods are dangerous to life and property for several reasons. First and foremost, floods kill more people in the U.S. per year than any other severe weather hazard. And regardless of one's ability to swim, floods pose a risk for everyone in any area that experiences this particular event. Oddly enough, most flood deaths in the U.S. occur in automobiles as people seek to avoid flood waters. Between the years 2006-2012, "a total of 147 citizens...drowned by floods."[2] This figure is based on a report issued by the Centers for Disease Control (CDC), which revealed that over half of all flood-related drownings occur when a vehicle is driven into hazardous flood water. The chief reason for these deaths is that most people underestimate the dangers of flood waters as they attempt to drive through them...until it is too late, and their automobiles are swept downstream.

Also what individuals fail to realize is that what looks to be a relatively "small" amount of water is really a force of deceptively incredible power. A 6-inch (15 ¼ centimeter) deep flood with a fast-moving current is capable of knocking an adult off their feet. A mere 2 feet (60 cm.) moving at 10 mph (16 km/h) can float most vehicles, including sports utility vehicles (SUVs) and pickup trucks. What's more, the majority of these in-car drowning deaths tend to occur at night, when visibility is at its lowest,

A woman in Athens, Greece clings to her vehicle in order to prevent being swept away by flood waters in February 2013. She was eventually rescued.

and the ability to underestimate the dangers at their highest.

---

[2] Adnan Turgut and Tevfik Turgut, "Floods and Drowning Incidents by Floods," World Applied Sciences Journal 16 (8): 1158-1162, 2012

   The risk of drowning in a flood while on foot is just as present as that for those who drown in automobiles. In fact, people walking into and through flood waters make up the second highest percentage of those who die from drowning...and for the same reasons as those who die in automobiles. Like those attempting to drive through flood waters, swiftly moving shallow water can be deadly, particularly for small children. This is because children have a tendency to play near areas where flood waters collect more readily, such as storm drains and irrigation ditches (such places are dangerous even in favorable weather conditions. When it rains, the water can accumulate very fast, creating a very strong current).

   Another reason floods are dangerous is because of the ecological and environmental damage they cause. Flooding tends to erode land, particularly the top soil on farmlands, which impacts food productivity. Furthermore, erosion from flooding around certain areas can release and spread chemical fertilizers, solvents, and other such products, potentially contaminating local water supply systems. Municipal and well water in affected flood areas often becomes undrinkable because of the presence of harmful bacteria and the other contaminants. The release of such chemical products can also have an adverse effect on local wildlife and their environs, especially fish. Related to this ecological damage is the often undesirable consequence of sewage release into groundwater supplies as well as on surrounding lands from overwhelmed drainage systems and household septic tanks. And because people are often forced to walk through floodwaters to reach safety, the increased toxicity of the water caused by the presence of raw sewage and other pollutants increases the chance of contact with waterborne pathogens (infectious germs). This is particularly true if open wounds are exposed to the contaminated water.

   A third reason that floods are dangerous is due to presence of hazardous foreign objects often found in floodwater. Primary among these hazards are broken and exposed utility conduits. These include gas and electrical lines. Flood waters often hide downed electrical lines, creating a potential electrocution hazard for those walking nearby. Broken and/or exposed gas lines can leak, creating a risk for explosions in the presence of an ignition source. In some cases, more long-term potential dangers can be exposed by flood waters. In 2011, flood-related erosion in the Missouri Basin of the near-Western mountain region of U.S. exposed two oil pipelines, resulting in their rupturing. A resulting oil leak in the pipes released over 1,500 barrels (238,481 liters) of oil into the Yellowstone River in Montana. And of course, there is the possibility of dangerous debris floating in flood waters. Splintered wood, nails, broken glass, and other assorted objects can tear and puncture skin.

   Along with the dangers from ruptured and broken utility conduits, flood waters often displace wild animals from their natural habitats. Animals displaced and exposed to flood waters often come into contact with people. In some areas, dangerous animals such as poisonous snakes, alligators, crocodiles, and poisonous insects represent an immediate hazard. Other displaced animals like raccoons, possums, and rodents might represent a rabies hazard if they are infected. Dead animals, stinging and biting insects (such as bees and disease-carrying mosquitoes) carry their own associated health risks. [3]

---

[3] Flooding, especially warmer climates often results in excessive breeding of mosquitoes. Swarms of mosquitoes may be seen in the affected regions several weeks after the storm. Such large numbers of mosquitoes means an increased probability of the presence of mosquitoes of the disease-carrying variety. In the U.S., the disease threat by vector mosquitoes includes West Nile virus, dengue fever, and various forms of encephalitis (such as the Western equine and St. Louis forms of the disease). Adding to the long-threat posed by flooding is the fact that mosquito eggs can lie dormant for an extended period of time without water, hatching years after their being laid.

And of course, there is the possibility of dangerous debris floating in flood waters. Splintered wood, nails, broken glass, and other assorted objects can tear and puncture skin. Waters contaminated with sewage, fuels, and other chemicals present an increased danger for those with open wounds; open cuts in the skin invite infections.

Even after flood waters recede there are other health risks that remain present. Long-term standing water, high levels of humidity, and wet materials are a breeding ground for microorganisms. Damp dwellings and furnishings promote the growth and proliferation of bacteria, dust mites, cockroaches and especially mold. Of all of these, molds are a particular cause for concern. Breathing in mold can lead to respiratory difficulties that include sinus infections and congestion. In addition, skin and eye irritation as well as coughing can also be a direct result of breathing in flood-spawned mold. According to the U.S. Environmental Protection Agency (EPA), individuals who already have a pre-existing lung disease or a compromised immune system may also be in danger of developing mold infection in the lungs. The moist conditions left behind by floods, particularly those found in damaged homes and buildings can generate a host of health concerns, including (but not limited to) aggravating existing asthma and allergies, the development of asthma, wheezing, coughing, and the potential for other health-related maladies such as *hypersensitivity pneumonitis*[4] for individuals who might be at risk.

Mold forming in a flooded-out home in the aftermath of Hurricane Katrina in New Orleans in 2005

Finally, and indirectly related to the dangers of hazardous debris in flood waters and environmental conditions inside flooded-out dwellings are the dangers presented by the dwelling themselves. Water in abundant amounts tends to damage homes and other primarily wood-constructed buildings. This is due to the softening (and subsequent weakening) of the structure that occurs to the submerged wood that makes up the frames of flood-exposed dwellings. This means that homes and buildings exposed to flood waters may become dilapidated and potentially uninhabitable, as they may collapse due to their

---

[4] Hypersensitivity pneumonitis is health condition characterized by an inflammation of lung tissue, caused by hypersensitivity to inhaled organic dusts or dust-like particles, such as flood mold.

weakened structures (and foundations). The result could be the total financial loss of a home or business, and a potential loss to human life should a human opt to inhabit one of these unsafe structures.

Flash floods carry with them their own set of unique dangers. The first of these dangers is their suddenness; flash floods tend to come with little or no prior warning. This fact increases the likelihood that injuries or even deaths might occur when they happen. Flash floods can occur within as few as a few minutes or a couple of hours of a heavy rainfall, a levee breach/dam failure, or a sudden release of water along a waterway (by definition, excessively accumulated water that occurs within a span of 3 hours or less is considered a flash flood). Depending on the magnitude of a particular flash flood, these sudden deluges of water can move heavy objects, uproot and move trees, and destroy homes and buildings that happen to be in their path. Furthermore, flash flood-producing rains can also trigger dangerous and catastrophic mud slides. Most flood deaths worldwide are due to flash floods.

Floods are dangerous because of the immediate and long-term risks to the health and lives of those who might be affected by them. They occur all over the world, inflicting death and destruction annually. In fact, floods are the most common natural disaster. They are the natural disaster that results in more deaths annually than any other natural disaster (with the exception of heat waves/droughts). They are also costly economically, causing in the multiples of billions of dollars in damage in the U.S. alone every year. This includes [the] direct damage and destruction of property as well as costs incurred in cleaning up flood damage, and the financial losses of businesses affected. Although floods generally occur over a gradual period, flash floods can occur in minutes—sweeping away cars, homes, livestock, even bridges (in addition to lives). Since most floods develop gradually, those who might be affected tend to have ample time to prepare or evacuate. For this reason, prior planning is key to surviving floods and their equally dangerous aftermaths.

KEY POINTS

- As much as 90% of property damage related to all natural disasters is caused by floods (and associated debris flows).

- Flooding is the most common type of natural disaster worldwide - 40% of all natural disasters.

- Floods are the number-one cause of weather-related deaths in both the United States, and the world.

Where Do Floods Occur?

Strictly speaking, there are very few places on Earth where flooding is not a concern. Floods can theoretically occur anyplace there is the potential for more rain (or a source of water) than there is for water to dissipate or drain. Although excessive rain is the direct cause of many floods, heavy rain itself is not the only impetus for a flood; floods can actually happen in a various ways. What's more, the overwhelming majority of floods occur on areas of land that are broad and flat, and usually situated on the banks of a river, lake, ocean, or some other waterway (or water source). These waterway-adjacent flat lands are called *floodplains* because of they are prone to flooding when the water levels of nearby bodies of water reach *flood stage* (the point at which a body of water has risen to a level high enough to cause inundation of normally dry land, and that is sufficient to threaten to property damage or loss of life).

Since the earliest civilizations, men have built both their individual homes as well as entire population centers near and on floodplains, where they are highly susceptible to flooding. Floodplains themselves can be limited to a small patch of land or encompass a very large region. Houses and communities that are built on floodplains often require greater insurance coverage due to the higher likelihood of flooding, as compared to that of homes established on land higher land elevations. In some cases, flooding on known floodplains occurs with oftentimes catastrophic regularity. In China for example, it has been estimated that the Yellow (Yangtze) River has flooded [the] various regions around the river's path over 1,500 times during its recorded history (since 602 B.C.), before the erection of modern dams on the river. The past flooding of the Yellow River includes some of the deadliest natural disasters ever recorded, giving it the dubious distinction of being the river that has taken the most lives anywhere in the world. In the U.S., the vast areas of surrounding lands that makes up the Mississippi and Missouri floodplains can and do become inundated when these powerful rivers overflow their banks, especially during infrequently heavy rain cycles. The various regions around these particular waterways are ringed with flood-control measures such as *dams*, *levees*, and *dikes* that allow communities to control the flooding of the rivers—thus mitigating and in some cases, preventing damage to local property. However, these flood management protocols can and *do* fail at times. Levees and dams can be overwhelmed during particularly intense weather events such as major rain events, hurricanes, and tropical storms—causing flooding that could potentially go beyond the boundaries of known floodplains.[5]

In the U.S., both populated and unpopulated areas along the *Mississippi River Basin* are situated on expansive floodplains that are linked together by the Mississippi river itself. This area is called a river "basin" (or *watershed*) because the Mississippi River –the longest and largest river in the U.S.–is also the largest natural drainage system on the North American continent, with other major (but smaller) rivers and waterways connected to it. In fact, the Mississippi River drains the majority of the area between the crest of the Rocky Mountains and parts of the Appalachian Mountains—approximately 40% of the total land areas of the continental United States! This means that when connecting major

---

[5] Floodplains are not to be confused with *floodways*, which are another engineered means of regulating flood waters. *Regulatory Floodways* (as they are also called) channel the waters of a river or other watercourse through adjacent land areas (areas reserved in order to discharge excessive accumulation of water without increasing the average normal height of the waterway's surface). Floodways are typically associated with [the normally] dry zones of lands between levees designated by local (or state) municipalities, and engineered to convey flood waters away from areas where they could threaten lives and/or property.

rivers to the Mississippi such as the Ohio and Missouri Rivers flood, the Mississippi River drains off the excessive water. Conversely, when the Mississippi itself floods, the connecting rivers may be forced to absorb excess waters, thus raising *their* water levels and triggering flood threats along *their* floodplains. It is because of this geographic structure that many areas along the Mississippi River, major connecting rivers, and *their* connecting *tributaries* (smaller streams, rivers, or waterways that flow into a main river or a lake) form the flood-prone region of the Mississippi River Basin in its entirety. At the same time, the major rivers within the Mississippi River Basin have their own individual flood prone river basins (e.g., the Missouri River and Ohio River Basins).

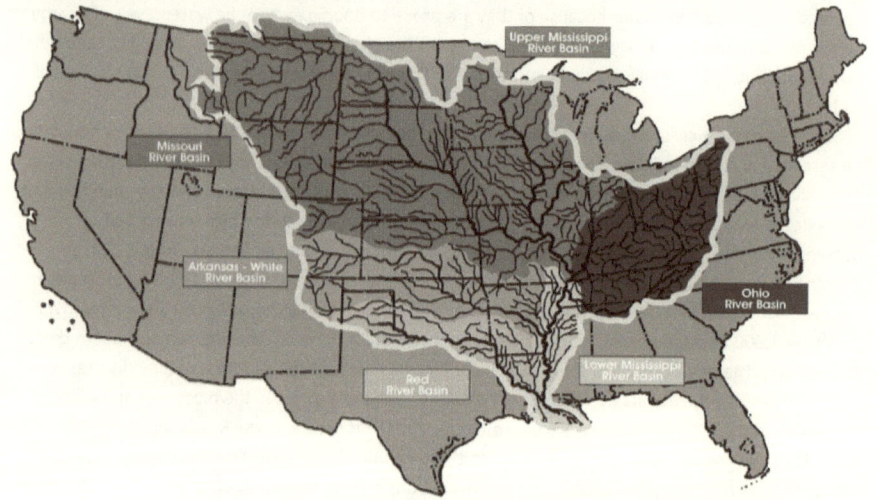

Map of Mississippi River Basin, connecting lesser basins, and its tributary structure

Although many established floodplains tend to usually flood during a region's flood (rainy) season, the potential for flooding in low-lined and other land areas are not limited to direct weather-based phenomena as a cause. As urban sprawl forces construction and development of previously uninhabited lands, rapid urbanization has led to more paving that covers the natural ground. Soils and plants are replaced with concrete and asphalt, which prevents water from draining naturally. An unusually heavy amount of rain can cause the pooling and accumulation of water, causing flooding of small (or large) patches of lands and nearby homes and businesses—especially those with basements. The upshot is that the development of, and encroachment on previously undeveloped lands can create artificial floodplains—creating a risk for flooding in areas that had previously not known a flood risk.

In other cases, a combination of nature and changes to the physical lay of the land wrought by man have created other areas where flooding is potential problems. The Netherlands, in Northern Europe is a country where nearly quarter of its population lives on land that lies below *sea level* (the average surface level of the oceans outside of the influence of the tides). That is because approximately half of the country's total land area also is below sea level (see map—right—with the shade representing the below sea-level portion of the land area). Part of the reason for this reality is because the earliest settlers of this country bordering on the North Sea established colonies on its low-lying shoreline ridges. Roman settlers later followed, building the first dam in the area to combat frequent flooding in the area. Still later, Christian monks arrived, building monasteries and protecting them with the first true dikes. With the invention of the windmill 600 years ago, the population was able expand living space by utilizing pumps to drain larger and larger areas of low-lying land of water from the bordering sea. But during earlier times, much of the land was found to have contained large amounts of *peat*.[6] In areas of Northern

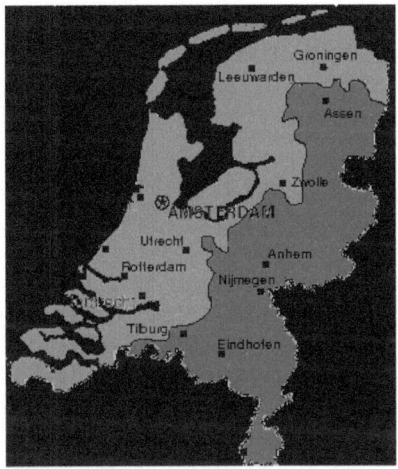

Europe—including the Netherlands peat—was extracted over an extended period of time in such large amounts that the height of the already low-laying land was lowered even more. In fact, the level of the land was lowered by an average of several feet/meters from peat extraction practices alone.

Land reclamation policies were put into place some time ago in order to counter the lowering of the land and protect the region from the increased potential flooding. These realities factored into the disastrous 1953 flood in the "low countries" region of Northern Europe that includes the Netherlands.

Several of the over 1,100 windmills found throughout the Netherlands, used to pump water from the land.

---

[6] Peat is a naturally-occurring material usually found in land areas that tend to have a high water—such as those in flood prone areas—and low oxygen content). Although not generally considered a true fossil fuel, peat was (and continues to be) harvested on an industrial scale, and used as a fuel and heat source primarily in European countries.

After the resulting 1,800 deaths and massive property damage, the country built the *Delta Works*. The Delta Works are an elaborate system of mechanical locks, dams, storm surge barriers, and other flood management mechanisms designed to close off the various waterway inlets from the land in the event of rising water levels that threaten to flood the land. In addition, the country has since continued to increase land availability by removing sea water from low-level lands once claimed by the North Sea.

In the U.S., the historic city of New Orleans is in a similar situation. About half of its land is either at or below sea-level, due primarily its location at the mouth of the Mississippi River on one side, and situated south of nearby Lake Pontchartrain on the other. And despite a similarly extensive series of flood-control mechanisms different from those established in the Netherlands, the city was devastated by floods in 2005 brought on by Hurricane Katrina. During the record-setting storm, the federally-built system of levees and floodwalls surrounding the city were breached by the rising waters of Lake Pontchartrain, causing some 80% of the city to become submerged (and over 1,500 lives lost). The United States Army Corp of Engineers (USACE)[7] has since rebuilt the city's elaborate flood-protection precautions.

However, even with anti-flood measures, land with a negative elevation (i.e., below sea level) like that found in and around the city of New Orleans and in the Netherlands is still prone to flooding. Likewise, open lands that are situated relatively low in relation to existing waterways adjacent to them—like those within the Mississippi Basin region—make these particular areas prone to flooding. In addition to the Mississippi River Basin, lands within lesser-known basins across the U.S. and in other countries are equally susceptible to potential flooding.

Just as many areas are prone to flash flooding. And some areas, much like in the case of overland flooding are more susceptible to flash flooding than others. In the U.S., the "monsoon season" of the desert Southwest tends to bring an increased probability of this danger. During the summer months of July and August, changes in wind flow patterns bring in streams of heavy moisture from the Pacific Ocean and the Gulf of Mexico. This moisture, in concert with the intense daytime heating which happens in the region tends to bring about a pattern of thunderstorms that produce heavy rains. These heavy rains often come with such ferocity and suddenness that a routine occurrence of flash floods is often the result. These flash floods can happen with such regularity that many areas of land in the region are scarred with naturally-occurring gullies and washes that mark the flow patterns of rapidly rushing water from these flash floods. Other areas across the globe that experience similar monsoon rain patterns are also vulnerable to flash flooding.

Finally, newly developed areas where the construction has altered the environment can result in flooding caused by changes occur to the natural drainage dynamics of such areas. As man continues to encroach into undeveloped areas—cutting down trees, paving new roadways and, building new subdivisions—less natural soil becomes available to absorb water. Moreover, some residential

---

[7] The United States Army Corp of Engineers (USACE) is an agency within federal government responsible for (among other responsibilities) building and maintaining vital public works projects. Specifically, the agency's mission is "to provide vital public engineering services in peace and war to strengthen the nation's security, energize the economy, and reduce risks from disasters." With regard to flood threats, the USACE is responsible for designing and constructing dams and canals, as well as the dredging of waterways in order to mitigate the potential for disruptions caused by a breakdown of these systems. Ultimately, the USACS) is responsible for policies involving flood protection with the borders of the U.S.

developments are built atop wet lands because such land is comparatively inexpensive compared to other areas. The result is that any accumulated water may then be left with no place to drain or sink into the earth, which in turn can cause a flood.

Forecasting and Measuring Flood Intensity/Frequency

Unlike tornadoes, earthquakes, and hurricanes, floods don't have a standardized rating system to measure the amount of damage and intensity per se. However, there are three standard factors that scientists apply to determining the scale of a flood: the *flood stage*, which is the (estimated or measured) depth of the water; the *discharge*, or amount of water that passes through a given area within a certain period; and the amount of land area covered by flood water. These factors play a role in the short-term forecasting, which allows precautions to be taken to prevent possible damage to property or loss of life in advance of potential flooding.

Flood designations as such, are based on statistical averages. They are the accumulation of long-term studies involving statistical models and other data that allows for distinctions between different flood events. For example, meteorologists will describe certain particularly extensive floods as a level of "multi-year flood" events, such as a "50-year flood event" or a "100-year flood event."[8] However, this label is somewhat misleading because it elicits thoughts of a particular flood occurring only once during such a timeframe (e.g., an individual might conclude that a "50-year flood" in a given area can only happen once every 50 years). Such terms are merely statistical designations meaning that, for example, a "50-year flood" equates to 1-in-50 chance that a flood of such size and scope will occur. But given the countless numbers of factors involving climatic patterns over a period of years as well as the laws of chance, the *actual* period of time that could pass between "50-year floods" could be as much as a century, or as little as a single year. Comparing the extensiveness and duration of a particular flood in addition to ever-shifting weather patterns, a 50- or 100- year flood could happen in successive years or once over a span of many years—not necessarily once within the presumed period of time suggested by a label. "Multi-year" flood events then are a designation used to describe the magnitude and extent of a particular flood, not as a given duration of time between such floods.

Furthermore, flood designations have a tendency to change over time. This is due to not only changing weather patterns, but changes in the physical environment of a floodplain or waterway basin. As scientists continue to study the environment, and more data are collected, they may note how small and/or a significant change in a waterway basin affects the flow of water. This may result in a re-evaluation of the frequency of flooding for such affected areas. The construction of water-control devices such as dams and urban development are examples of some man-made changes in a basin that affect flood patterns.

Government agencies use such studies to predict the likelihood of flooding for a given area. In the U.S., the Federal Emergency Management Agency (FEMA)[9] uses such criteria to designate federally-

---

[8] Although flooding is often hear described in terms of "multi-year" events such as a "quarter-century/25-year flood," a "30-year flood," or a "half-century/50-year flood," the "100-year flood" is the statistical standard used by FEMA and other concerned interests. The 100-year flood is the basis that such agencies use in order to describe a particularly extensive flood event as well as calculate the probability for such an event to occur at the same level over a given period of time.

[9] FEMA (Federal Emergency Management Agency) is a federal agency established to respond to major emergencies that state and local agencies don't have the resources to handle. FEMA seeks to reduce the loss of life and protect property against all types of hazards through a comprehensive, risk-based emergency management program.

recognized *flood zones*. Flood zones are FEMA-recognized land areas that describe such areas in terms of their frequency of, and overall risk for experiencing flooding. Based on the varying levels of criterion used by FEMA, everyone lives in a flood zone—it's just a question of whether individuals live in a low, moderate, or high risk area. Land areas at higher elevations and/or in drier climates tend to be less prone to flooding (although the probability in both cases is not zero). Coastal areas and identified river/waterway basins on the other hand tend to be in the highest risk zones for flooding. These zones are also recognized and used by insurance companies to calculate flood risks and projected insurance rates for issuing property coverage insurance (see the FEMA Flood Zone Designation chart below for an explanation of how each flood zone is defined).

The next 2 pages list the various FEMA Flood Zone Designations by individual definitions, and their related risk levels. These zones are identified on a community's Flood Insurance Rate Map (FIRM) or Flood Hazard Boundary Map. Each zone reflects the severity or type of flooding in the area eligible for protection under the National Flood Insurance Program (NFIP).

Moderate to Low Risk Areas In communities that participate in the NFIP, flood insurance is available to all property owners and renters in these zones:

ZONE	DESCRIPTION
B and X (shaded)	Area of moderate flood hazard, usually the area between the limits of the 100-year and 500-year floods. Are also used to designate base floodplains of lesser hazards, such as areas protected by levees from 100-year flood, or shallow flooding areas with average depths of less than one foot or drainage areas less than 1 square mile.
C and X (unshaded)	Area of minimal flood hazard, usually depicted on FIRMs as above the 500-year flood level.

High Risk Areas In communities that participate in the NFIP, mandatory flood insurance purchase requirements apply to all of these zones:

ZONE	DESCRIPTION
A	Areas with a 1% annual chance of flooding and a 26% chance of flooding over the life of a 30-year mortgage. Because detailed analyses are not performed for such areas; no depths or base flood elevations are shown within these zones.
AE	The base floodplain where base flood elevations are provided. AE Zones are now used on new format FIRMs instead of A1-A30 Zones.
A1-30	These are known as numbered A Zones (e.g., A7 or A14). This is the base floodplain where the FIRM shows a BFE (old format).
AH	Areas with a 1% annual chance of shallow flooding, usually in the form of a pond, with an average depth ranging from 1 to 3 feet. These areas have a 26% chance of flooding over the life of a 30-year mortgage. Base flood elevations derived from detailed analyses are shown at selected intervals within these zones.

AO	River or stream flood hazard areas, and areas with a 1% or greater chance of shallow flooding each year, usually in the form of sheet flow, with an average depth ranging from 1 to 3 feet. These areas have a 26% chance of flooding over the life of a 30-year mortgage. Average flood depths derived from detailed analyses are shown within these zones.
AR	Areas with a temporarily increased flood risk due to the building or restoration of a flood control system (such as a levee or a dam). Mandatory flood insurance purchase requirements will apply, but rates will not exceed the rates for unnumbered A zones if the structure is built or restored in compliance with Zone AR floodplain management regulations.
A99	Areas with a 1% annual chance of flooding that will be protected by a Federal flood control system where construction has reached specified legal requirements. No depths or base flood elevations are shown within these zones.

High Risk - Coastal Areas In communities that participate in the NFIP, mandatory flood insurance purchase requirements apply to all of these zones:

ZONE	DESCRIPTION
V	Coastal areas with a 1% or greater chance of flooding and an additional hazard associated with storm waves. These areas have a 26% chance of flooding over the life of a 30-year mortgage. No base flood elevations are shown within these zones.
VE, V1 - 30	Coastal areas with a 1% or greater chance of flooding and an additional hazard associated with storm waves. These areas have a 26% chance of flooding over the life of a 30-year mortgage. Base flood elevations derived from detailed analyses are shown at selected intervals within these zones.

Undetermined Risk Areas

ZONE	DESCRIPTION
D	Areas with possible but undetermined flood hazards. No flood hazard analysis has been conducted. Flood insurance rates are commensurate with the uncertainty of the flood risk.

When the flood risk of the various FEMA-recognized and designated flood zones are placed in the context of graphic measuring the risk for flooding in-relation to the a particular zone, the zones and associated risks play out like the following:

MODERATE	LOW RISK AREAS	HIGH RISK AREAS	HIGH RISK COASTAL AREAS	UNDETERMINED RISK AREAS	
C and X (unshaded)	B and X (shaded)	A, AE, A1-30, AH, AO, A99	V, VE, V1-30	D	

Flood Zone Designations

In the United Kingdom, flood forecasting is administered by the Flood Forecasting Centre (FFC). The FFC is a government agency that utilizes the combined technological resources and meteorological expertise of two other government agencies, the Environmental Agency and The Meteorological Office (also known as the MET Office). Working together, these agencies promote the communication of advisories of flood risk that enables national and local responders to take steps to protect life and property. Similarly in the United States, flood forecasts are issued by the National Weather Service (NWS) and supported by 13 regional NWS-affiliated specialty offices known collectively as the River Forecast Centers.

When particular conditions exist such as the potential for an excessive level of rainfall, agencies like the NWS closely begin to monitor these conditions as well as their potential for creating a flood threat more closely. For example, when rain is expected to begin falling for an extended period of time or at a particular intensity level, these agencies might take note that the water runoff may not immediately drain off into a river or stream. If the runoff is projected to fail to flow into the river (or other waterway) within the amount of time needed for the affected area to properly drain (within a basin), or if excessive amounts of water drains into waterways with a threat of causing an overflow of the waterway's banks, a series of related weather advisories might be issued. These include:

- Urban/Small Stream/Flood Advisory – Is an advisory alerting the public to flooding which is generally considered an inconvenience, and not a moderate or significant threat to life and/or property. This is typical issued when a heavy or extensive rain event is expected to cause flooding of streets and low-lying places in urban areas. It is also issued when small rural or urban streams are expected to reach or exceed their banks. However, some minor damage to homes or roads could occur under worse scenario conditions.

- Flood Watch – is an advisory issued for an affected area whenever current and/or developing weather patterns indicate a potential for gradual flooding that may be widespread. Although the occurrence of actual flooding may or may not be, a flood watch should be taken as an advisory to residents, local government agencies, and other local interests in the watch area to consider reviewing flood action plans. The watch should also be trigger closer observation of changing weather conditions, and preparations to act should a flood warning be issued.

- Flood Warning - is an advisory normally issued for flooding that is either occurring or imminent. Because flood warnings are based on expectation of [the] gradual development of flooding, it is usually issued in response to the threat of prolonged and/or persistent, (moderate to heavy) rainfall that is predicted to result in the buildup of water in low-lying, flood prone areas. Flood warnings may also be issued when creeks, streams, and/or rivers are expected to flood over their banks, especially in areas that may affect property and lives (despite the propensity for this type of flooding to develop more slowly than flash flooding, the threat to life and property is always a possibility).

- Flash Flood Watch – is a type of advisory issued when the potential for flash flooding is a possibility within or close to the watch area. A flash flood watch should be considered an alert for those in the affected area to be ready to take action if a flash flood warning is issued or flooding is observed. These particular watches are issued whenever flooding is expected to occur less than 6 hours after a (moderate to heavy) rainfall event, and may cover a large area. A Flash Flood Watch may also be issued whenever there exist a potential for a levee breach or a dam break to occur. In rare cases, they may also be issued during torrential rains, or whenever there is a known ice jam on a river, particularly during late winter or early spring thaws.

- Flash Flood Warning – is an advisory issued for flooding usually occurring within 6 hours of a heavy rain event, which typically results in small creeks and streams quickly rising beyond the boundaries of their banks. Dangerous floods in areas near these creeks and streams (as well as low-lying flood prone areas) have a tendency to develop very quickly, and can be a significant threat to life and/or property.

Flood forecasting, although far from perfect has advanced throughout the last 2 centuries to the point where at least advisories can be competently issued whenever there is a realistic threat to life and/or property from threatening flood waters. Watches and warnings can be competently issued for rural or urban areas as well as for areas along the major rivers. Even set-up conditions for hard-to-predict flash floods can be anticipated by weather forecasting agencies, providing warning to those who might be threatened whenever heavy rainfall or other casual factors are at play. Flood forecasting takes into consideration various contributing factors to the potential for flooding, including: the amount of expected participation (i.e., rain); the overall period of time rainfall is expected; the geography of the local terrain; previous ground saturation (if it exist); degree of urbanization and related development; alterations to waterways due to development or natural geographical changes over time; and initial ground or river conditions.

Flood Regulation Methods to Reduce Vulnerability

Some of the more flood-prone regions, especially those in industrialized Western nations like the U.S., are not totally at the mercy of flood waters. Low-lying land, especially those where major population centers are situated are often protected by various flood-control measures. Most of these measures are designed to either reduce the extent of impending flooding, alleviate the pressure of rising waters in order to prevent massive flooding, or hold back potential flood waters from places where both people and property are located. While there is truly no way to eradicate flooding from any major waterway, some engineering feats have been more effective at controlling flooding than others.

In some low-lying regions with a particular vulnerability to flooding, flood management systems include the use of *floodgates*. Also known as "crest gates," floodgates are mechanisms designed to allow for the controlled flow of water from the various types of waterways. These gated structures operate by remaining open during regular waterway levels, especially on waterways in which boats and ships navigate. When high tides, storm surges, or heavy rains threaten to raise the normal water levels, the gates closed in order to reduce the risk of flooding to nearby dry and populated land. At other times, gates may be opened to release excess water that rises above normal levels. When the threatening rising waters recede to a safe level, the gates are reopened and normal drainage resumes. The best example of floodgates can be seen within the Netherlands Delta Works project. Gates which comprise part of the Works' elaborate flood control system close or open, based on potential flood threats.

The Maeslant Barrier near Rotterdam, Netherlands, part of the country's Delta Works system of flood control, is a set of massive floodgates along the Nieuwe Waterweg waterway, which protects land below sea-level from the water of the bordering North Sea.

In addition to being part of a larger flood control apparatus, floodgates are often built as part of large retention dams, or as a component of some reservoirs. But floodgates can fail at critical moments. A highly-destructive earthquake struck the island nation of Japan in 2011, triggering an equally destructive tsunami (a fast-moving wall of destructive water). As the tsunami brought on catastrophic flooding in coastal areas of the country, at least one floodgate near the coastal town of *Rikuzentakata* failed to close. This allowed rushing water to charge into the area unchallenged, virtually wiping the town off the map and contributing to the near 16,000 deaths caused by the tsunami and resulting flooding.

Similar to floodgates, *flood sluices* are a form of flood control that allows for the control of water flow. They are usually found at the opening of a flood "sluiceway." Sluiceways are typically manmade (but not exclusively) channels that allow for the controlled flow of water in a given direction when a *sluice gate* is opened. The gate can be controlled at the site of the gate or remotely. And while materials such as brick, concrete, wood, and metal can all be used in the construction of these typically

artificial channels, natural channels may be enhanced by a combination of digging and artificially reinforcing their linings to improve their use as a flood control measure. The problem with sluices—both manmade and natural—is that they usually require routine maintenance. In some cases, some type of screening may be used to keep debris out of the channel. On occasion, the water flow within a sluice channel may need to be halted in order to allow for engineers and/or personnel responsible to maintaining its function to enter the sluice to remove silt and other foreign material. This process is also used for checking for and damaged components that may need replacement.

The Lat Chado **sluice gate** is one of three Ayutthaya's Pak Hai district in Thailand

Lack of maintenance funds, neglect, or simply failure to perform regular maintenance on sluice gates can result in problems such as mechanical failure—which can result in local flooding. Such an operational failure of a sluice gate occurred in 2006 in Washington State. The gates at the Cowlitz Falls Hydroelectric Project near the city of Randle failed to close during a flood that year, resulting in were $1 million in damage to the Project facilities.

Flood pumps and pumping stations are yet another means for local emergency personnel and responsible agencies to manage flooding in threatened areas. Pumping stations (including the actual pumps therein) are facilities that function to removal flood waters from flooded lands, and are usually operated by local municipalities. Depending on the particular geographic lay of the land, municipal flood pumps may function slightly different. Pumps operating to drain low-lying lands of water accumulation may pump excess water/flood waters into *drainage canals* or *drainage ditches* (artificially-constructed channels used to drain water from an area having no natural outlet for precipitation/water accumulation). In most instances, when pumping stations are designed to pump flood waters from areas below sea level, it usually becomes necessary to pump the water upwards and out into waterways that eventually drain into a river, reservoir, or some other type of waterway. An example of this type of pumping station setup is those that comprise the flood defenses in and around the city of New Orleans. Because a great portion of the city lies below sea level, it relies on manually-operated pumps to remove rain and flood waters through a series of canal into nearby Lake Pontchartrain, which sits elevated in relation to the city. Additionally, in the wake of the catastrophic flooding caused by Hurricane Katrina, the USACE replaced and rebuilt and replaced the older pumping stations which served the city, but which were overwhelmed the flood waters from the 2005 storm.

The exterior and interior of the Warren Creek Pumping Station, in Mankato, Minnesota. The station houses three large water pumps that operate as part of the city's flood control plan. The Warren Creek Station is one of 5 in the city situated near the city, which at the intersection of the Blue Earth and Minnesota Rivers.

Even outside of extreme events such like Hurricane Katrina, pumps and other mechanisms to control flooding can fail. During early July of 2013 pumping stations serving Panama City, Florida failed to operate during moderately heavy rains, causing damage to home along nearby Lake Huntington (although the exact reason for the pumps' failures were unexplained, it was suspected that the problems were caused by a critical electrical component in the pumps).

Another form of flood control is a dam. Dams are used primarily for retaining water. When they are built along reservoirs, they are also used to store collected water. Water stored by dams can be managed with a controlled flow, which can then be evenly distributed between different locations along a waterway, or used to generate hydroelectric power. Many large dams have flood-control reservations by which the water levels of a reservoir must be kept below a certain height. In some instances, groups of dams built on along the moving waterways, with larger dams erected along the headwaters of moving waterways. This allows better management of potential floodwaters from excessive rainfall or melting snows that might fill the reservoir. Before the construction and completion of the Aswan High Dam in 1970 the Nile River in Egypt experienced predictable yearly summer flooding of the vital farmland located at the mouth of the river. This flooding

The Aswan High Dam, near Cairo, Egypt

was a particular problem for the desert country's increasing population, which required a commensurate increase in more land usage to grow more food. But these potentially fertile agricultural lands were claimed by the river's annual flooding. The Aswan Dam, built across the river some 600 miles (965 km) south of the capital city of Cairo, has effectively stopped the river's annual floods by trapping its waters in a reservoir. This water is then slowly released during the dry season, which now allows year-around planting of vital food crops in the region.

Countries like the U.S., with its abundance of waterways tend to have many more dams. According to the National Inventory of Dams, there are more than 79,000 dams in the U.S., with some 17,500 (and reservoirs) within the Missouri River Basin alone. Although most of these dams are small local irrigation structures along various tributaries of the river, there are 6 major dams that on the river proper that generate electricity, while providing control of the river's often devastating floods. Similar dam setups can be found within the other river basins that comprise the total Mississippi River Basin, many designed to prevent or mitigate potential flooding within these individual regions. But dams are not foolproof measures against floodwaters. In 2011 all 6 major dams along the Missouri River released record amounts of snowmelt and record rainfall-sourced water in an effort to prevent water overflow, which led to flooding in towns and cities in 6 different states connected to the river.

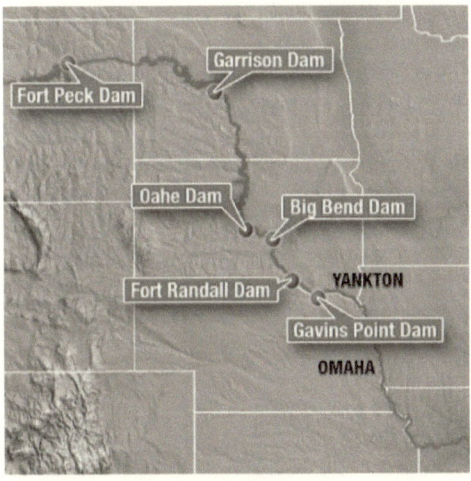

The 6 major dams erected along the Missouri River

In addition to multi-purpose dams, other flood-control measures in flood-prone regions include the use of levees and dikes. Levees/dikes, simply put are physical ridges which are raised higher than both the waterway they are bounded by, and the surrounding floodplains. In effect, levees and dikes serve as physical barrier designed to separate the land of floodplains from waterway, and prevent the flooding of lands that lay adjacent to the river, lake, or ocean that they border. They can be of the man-made type, composed of concrete or dry-stone walls or erected earthen barriers made of strengthened stone rocks, sand, or even dirt—all designed to be relatively permanent barriers against rising water. Additionally, levees can be of the type made of bags filled with sand. These latter types are usually temporary fortifications of existing (or non-existing) barriers meant to protect local land and property in times of immediate flood threats.

The region along the Mississippi River floodplain is comprised of a patchwork of levees of various designs and compositions. And like flood-prone areas of the Netherlands, this system of smaller levees tends to be constructed, owned, and maintained by the various local municipalities whom they immediately serve. These include the various towns, cities, and even privately- owned and maintained levees on private properties in and around the Mississippi Floodplain. Some of these levees protect entire towns, while others protect individual properties such as farms. Many of these levees are made of materials like concrete, sand, clay, dirt and other lesser known materials. There are in fact so many levees in this particular region of the U.S. that many smaller private levees, particularly those on the smaller rivers and streams connected to the Mississippi, are often forgotten.

In addition to the many individual levees around the Mississippi Floodplain, the river itself is protected by the Mississippi River and Tributaries (MR&T) project. This system of levees and floodways (see footnote on page 5) is the world's largest flood control project, even dwarfing the Netherlands' Delta Works. The MT&T project comprises a continuous 3,500 mile (5,632 km) long levee system constructed of compacted soil and clay. The system's levees were designed to protect areas of the region around the Mississippi River from destructive flooding by confining the flow of rising water to levied channels. While some MT&T levees lay along the Mississippi River itself, another near 600 miles/965 km lie along the south banks of the Arkansas and Red rivers and within their adjoining river basins.

However, no levee regardless of how sturdy and reliably it is constructed is fully flood-proof. These ramparts are meant solely to reduce the risk of flooding, not eliminate it entirely. Levees in fact are designed and constructed to retain a *certain amount* of water. Against limited and/or moderate flood threats, they may prove successful in preventing the inundation of nearby floodplains and the resulting damage to property. In such an instance, sandbags may be used to further insure protection against impending flood threats. In 1993, 2008, and 2011, the levees along the Mississippi and its various tributaries were easily overwhelmed by categorically major—catastrophic in the case of 1993—flooding of the Mississippi caused primarily by unusually heavy rainfall following a heavy snow-melt. In 2005 during height of Hurricane Katrina's rampage along the Gulf Coast of the U.S., levees protecting the city of New Orleans were not only breached by overtopping waters but had actually broken at more than 50 different points. This collective breaching was the direct cause of the flooding which inundated many areas of the city that lie below sea-level. Against major and catastrophic flood threats, levees—even fortified—are usually of little protection against such flood waters (similarly dikes, distinguished by their use along coastal regions bordering oceans and seas, can easily be overran by intense enough floodwaters caused by tidal surges...and are not usually fortified with sandbags.

Many of these major flood control measures operate in conjunction with other measures to prevent the flooding of populated areas in best-case scenarios, and mitigate the extent of flooding in worse-case scenarios. Along with flood channels, canals, and waterway *dredging* (the excavation of rivers and streams to increase water flow), communities—those with the resources—around the globe have sought to fight the threat of flooding for centuries. However, those measures are far from perfect or even fully effective, subject to either manmade failures or simply being overwhelmed by the powerful forces of nature. The upshot is then that the presence of mechanical and/or natural flood control measures within flood-prone regions should not convey an absolute sense of security and assurance, as these measures—no matter how extensive and elaborate—cannot guarantee a safeguard against potential floods. Any sense of false assurance adopted by the presence of flood control measures, or the idea that a particular area is safe from floods is where the potential for flood-related injuries, deaths, and property destruction becomes an issue.

Unfortunately, there are still a few instances, particularly those involving flash floods and flood events in underdeveloped regions where these disasters continue to be a threat. Even in developed countries like the U.S., floods kill more people every year than both tornadoes and hurricanes. However, flood forecasting in many developed regions has made enough steady advances to the point where dangerous floods can be anticipated, and measures can be taken to protect both lives and property from water-related harm.

One of the many levee breaches that occurred in New Orleans during 2005's Hurricane Katrina.

The No-Nonsense Guide To Flood Safety

What To Be On The Alert For...

Like most natural disasters, every flood is unique unto itself; the individual factors converging to create a flood disaster can be as varied as dangers lurking in the flood waters themselves. In one instance a flood could occur in a particular area where there had never been a history of any previous flooding. Bu due to gradual environmental changes such as soil erosion or the development of a population center, this area might begin to suddenly experience a flood after a single heavy rain event. In another instance, a flood may be expected due to predictable seasonal weather patterns such as those in monsoon-prone areas. Still in other areas, a sudden dam burst, reservoir leak, or construction accidental could result in a sudden flash flood. Overall when weather conditions warrant, the water levels of rivers and other waterways predisposed to rising over their banks are monitored closely. Under warranted conditions, meteorologists and other forecasters begin looking for any tell-tale signs that might signal an impending flood threat, and issue a community and/or weather advisory to that effect.

Flood/flash flood watches are issued when rainfall, intense weather conditions, or water-related events might cause creeks, streams and/or rivers to overflow their banks and onto surrounding lands. Whenever these mostly-weather advisories are issued, individuals in the affected watch area should begin monitoring weather conditions, as well as make themselves aware of local river and waterway levels. Generally, these watches are updated every 6-8 hours until the threat of flooding has ended, or a *flood warning* is issued. When flood watches are issued:

- The presence of torrential rains (including thunder and lightning), steady rains occurring for an extended period of time, or a combination of steady of heavy rains and rising water levels on rivers and streams—especially upstream—should be noted. Should these conditions be observed, residents should be ready to evacuate, if necessary.
- Residents living in low-lying areas or near a body of water should begin monitoring local radio and/or television stations (in addition to monitoring internet- and weather radio-based weather alerts) for continuous updates of conditions.
- The location of higher ground and/or designated shelters should be reviewed; with preparations to relocate to these areas of relative safety should waters suddenly begin to rise.
- If actual flooding is observed, it should be reported to the proper authorities, such as local emergency management offices or law enforcement agencies.

A Flood/Flash flood warning is issued when creeks, streams and/or rivers are in the process of actually flooding over their banks, or when flooding is imminent. These warnings are updated at least once a day until water levels drop below what's considered the *flood stage* (the point where the normal water levels of rivers, streams, or other waterways rise beyond their recognized boundaries and begin to cover areas of land not normally covered by waters), or when the threat for flooding had ended. When flood warnings are issued:

- Recognize that flood waters, especially during flash flooding, may rise quickly and that anyone in a warning area may only have as little as a few minutes to flee to should an evacuation be ordered.

- Rising water levels and/or the observation that water is starting to cover land areas which were previously dry should be noted.
- During an intense weather event such as a hurricane or other tropical system, a flood warning will almost always be issued due to the unusual but predictable amount of torrential rains such systems generate.
- In some rare instances, the water levels in a reservoir or behind a dam may become too high to safely and continually retain. In such cases, floodgates may need to be opened to relieve high accumulated water levels. This may at times cause controlled flooding in affected areas. If the flooding of an area is imminent due to the release of water through a floodgate, a warning siren will usually be sounded, indicating the imminent release of potentially flooding water. Such a circumstance should be treated in the same way that a flash flood situation is treated—as an indication that an evacuation is advised from affected areas.
- Those in the affected warning area(s) should be prepared evacuate to higher ground, especially if an evacuation order is given. At the very least, affected persons should remove themselves from areas subject to flooding such as dips, low spots, canyons, washes, and areas along streams and creeks. In urban areas, individuals should stay clear of clogged storm drains and under-passes (heavy water can quickly accumulate in these enclosed areas and create drowning hazards, especially for automobiles in flooded underpasses).

A *coastal flood watch* is a special type of weather advisory that is issued when the possibility exists for flooding of areas around and adjacent to waterway coastlines (e.g., a very large lake, an ocean, or sea) within a period of between 12 to 36 hours. This is especially true in cases of approaching squall lines or other strong weather fronts along the coasts of large lakes (e.g., any of the Great Lakes in the Northern U.S.), and approaching tropical weather systems such as tropical storms and hurricanes along lands bordering the ocean.

- The monitoring of weather reports tracking approaching storms and their projected paths should begin.
- Rising water or water starting to cover land areas which were previously dry prior to any storms or inclimate weather should be noted and reported.
- Contact local emergency management personnel or law enforcement should coastal flooding becomes evident.

A *coastal flood warning* is a weather advisory issued whenever areas in and around coastal regions are expected to become, or have become, flooded by sea water driven in typically by particularly intense weather events such as tropical storms or hurricanes. During such storms, a coastal flood warning will almost always be issued. In addition, such storm systems tend to generate *storm surges* (the rise in water levels over land driven by the high winds that accompany certain tropical storm systems), which create wind-driven flooding in affected areas.

When flood-related watches and warnings are issued, it should be a signal to those in the affected watch/warning areas to increase their vigilance and begin looking for indications of a possible or an imminent flood. Although it doesn't imply that people should look up at the sky every 5 minutes for torrential rains, it *does* mean that people should make themselves aware of changing weather conditions, or changes in their physical environments. In addition, knowing the location of safer (or elevated) lands as well as the safest route of travel by which to take in advance of floods and flooding conditions is the best means for ensuring that lives are saved in the event of a flood.

The damage from storm surge flooding on the Bolivar Peninsula in Texas from the 2008 landfall of Hurricane Ike.

How To Prepare In The Event Of A Flood...

As with any level of natural disaster, preparation is the key to saving lives and loss of valuable property in a flood emergency. This is especially true for those living on moderately to highly active floodplains. With the reality of flooding ever-present for high-risk flood zones, preparation is the key to survival and a quick recovery from the disruption to daily life that floods tend to cause. For those living in high-risk flood zones or coastal regions, the first suggested course of action is the purchase of flood insurance.

Flood Insurance

Flood insurance is not like other types of property-related insurance. It is usually not a part of not regular homeowners' insurance policies, which typically insures against property damage from circumstances such as house fires, storm damage, and toppled trees. Flood insurance is in fact a separate and specialized policy that is purchased through and administered by local insurance agents, but funded by the federal government (FEMA). In most cases, flood insurance is purchased as a separate policy usually from the same company that homeowners purchase their primary property insurance coverage. But in purchasing flood insurance, policyholders should be aware that flood policy coverage takes approximately 30 days to take effect. So factoring in this time gap in relation to the start of "flood seasons" or flood events should be considered. And as one would expect with any type of insurance, higher risks (for flooding) means higher the costs for the policy. From country to country, this aspect of flood insurance varies—if it is even an issue of coverage. In the UK for example, those living in high-risk flood areas are required by insurers to take steps to make their homes more flood-resistant, lest they face higher payments for coverage (premiums). In Canada, flood insurance doesn't exist.

But as convenient—and sometimes necessary—as flood insurance is to have for flood-threatened homeowners, it should be noted that there are some important coverage issues property-owners need to be aware of. This first is the understanding that flood policies do not provide financial re-imbursements for flood damage to basements (other than damage to heating, air conditioning, and/or water systems). This could be an issue in itself if those looking to purchase a flood insurance policy tend to store important items in their basements—even more problematic basements serve as center of high-use for activities such as recreation or expensive hobbies. On a related note, flood insurance policies also do not reimburse the cash value of damaged items. Instead, this type of insurance pays the cost of replacement items. Finally, flood insurance differs from traditional homeowners' insurance in that these policies *do not* pay for possible necessary and temporary relocation costs, such as hotels or apartments (that are often incurred as homeowners await repairs on damaged homes that may be temporarily uninhabitable). Flood-insurance claims are usually filed with the insurance company policy-holders purchased the policy.

Create A Flood Emergency Plan

For those living on floodplains or in moderate to high risk coastal flood zones, contingency planning for flooding should be a given the increased consideration. Flood emergency plans should be based on anticipating and mitigating potential problems that might arise in the event of a potential flood emergency. Among the anticipated steps to consider in preparing for floods are:

- Knowing the designated flood shelters and emergency relief centers for a given area *beforehand*. Also, any designated evacuation or emergency travel routes (to these locations) should be known as well (obviously, these routes should not be prone to flooding themselves). This information can be obtained from local (city or state/provincial) emergency management personnel or appropriate government agencies (or their posted websites). Knowing this information could save a great deal of confusion in the event that family members or other loved-ones become separated; each family member would know where to go in the event of a flood-related evacuation order. This information also helps in providing a quick exit from flood dangers in the event that a quick evacuation is needed (remember, flash floods can happen in a relatively short timeframe). In some areas, it may be necessary to know the location of higher ground in the event of certain kinds of flooding events.
  In addition, it's always a good idea to have an out-of-town relative or other contact (who everyone knows) that evacuees or separated loved-ones can either contact or plan to rendezvous with in the event of an evacuation.
- People should acquaint themselves aware of the general emergency plans for their community as well as their children's' schools, and places of employment, particularly as such plans relate to flood emergencies.
- Know the shelter rules for the temporary boarding of pets and make preparations for adhering to these rules. Check with local emergency contingency shelters as to whether they allow family pets to be sheltered along with owners (the legal exceptions to pets being barred entrance into shelters with families/individuals in many cases are in the case of animal "assistants," such as guide dogs for the blind). Pre-arrangements might have to be made with local animal shelters. If separation from a family pet is not desired, an alternative is to locate more distant shelters that may allow for animals to be temporarily housed with families/owners.
- Consider relocating or moving expensive and/or irreplaceable items in homes and businesses to safer locations. Move electronics, furniture, and other valuable items out of basements to prevent their damage or loss to flood waters. If important and/or delicate items are not too cumbersome or heavy, they might be relocated to a higher flood within a home, or to a storage unit out of harm's way. Moreover, hazardous materials (such as paint, oil, pesticides, and cleaning supplies) should also be either be moved to locations out of the way of flood waters, or waterproofed to prevent them from becoming contaminants in flood situations. Outside possessions should be brought indoors, or tied down securely. This includes lawn furniture, garbage cans, and other potentially mobile objects.
- If possible, small furnaces, water heaters, and electrical units should be either elevated or moved to a higher level in the home/dwelling. Utilities such as gas and should be disconnected in the event of an actual flood. Electrical appliances should be disconnected if flooding becomes imminent. Also, anyone wet or standing in water should avoid touching electrically-powered appliances
- Important documents should be kept at-hand for easy transport in the event of a mandated evacuation. Important documents such as insurance papers, medical records, bank account numbers, and birth certificates should be kept in a damaged-(or at the very least water-)

resistant container as a matter of general principle. Having these important items together close at-hand will save time gathering them in the event of an emergency. Having these items gathered together will also help in the recovery from disruption in livelihood flooding causes in the expected dealings with the various bureaucracies and agencies that will need such information as they try to assist recovery.

- The use of sandbags and where to secure (or purchase) them ahead of need-time is not only encouraged but advised in some cases. Sandbags can play an important role in keeping potentially damaging floodwaters from direct contact with property, especially on river floodplains. In many cases, constructing temporary sandbag levees as a barrier between rising river waters and threatened property have made the difference between being able to return to unscathed property and a total financial loss. [10]
- If an evacuation order is given, affected individuals (and their families) should be leave as soon as possible, putting flood emergency plans into effect. An emergency flood kit (see below) containing food and other items should be taken with any evacuation.

Build a flood disaster emergency kit

Determining the items necessary to sustain the health and life of individuals affected by flood emergencies should be a factor in considering whether to purchase or create a flood emergency kit. Because a flood emergency kit might have to accompany evacuees to an evacuation shelter, it should be limited in the amount of items it contains. Suggested items (based on anticipated needs) for a flood emergency kit should include the following items:

- Water. An estimated 1 gallon (about 3 ½ liters) of water for each person, per day (enough for at last 3 days) should be stored. In lieu of this suggested amount, bottled water can be purchased in cases for easy storage and accessibility in times of need during a flood emergency
- Food. A 2-3 day supply of non-perishable food. Because it's possible that electricity and other utilities might be disrupted during a flood emergency, foods that require neither refrigeration nor cooking are the best candidates for use in an emergency kit. Canned meats such as tuna and beef (jerky) and canned vegetables are good choices.
- A can opener for food (if canned goods are packed with the kit).
- A battery-powered or hand crank radio and extra batteries.
- An extra cell phone (prepaid or contract), battery, and/or charger.
- Tools such as wrench or pliers (as a means to turn off utilities).
- A flashlight (and extra batteries) or a kerosene-based enclosed lantern (and matches/a lighter) if extended periods of power loss are expected.
- A first aid kit. A simple first-aid kit can be purchased at mostly any "big box" store, or can be created from scratch based on anticipated needs. A simple first-aid kit should contain bandages (the plastic adhesive, rolled cloth, and/or the "liquid" varieties), roller cloth bandages, sterile

---

[10] In cases where there is an ongoing or present flood threat (such as when a river is known to be rising to threatening levels), the USACE, local emergency management, or particular offices of local government will either distribute sandbags, arrange for their distribution, or have information about obtaining them. See the appendix for information on how to use sandbags to shore up property against the threat of rising flood waters.

gauze pads, towelette wipes, medical tape, a liquid antiseptic (e.g., alcohol and/or peroxide), anti-bacterial soap, smelling salts, petroleum jelly, and latex gloves.

- Toilet paper and/or paper towels.
- Sleeping bags and/or extra thick blankets that could double as an impromptu sleeping surface/mat.
- Flood/damage control items. Under some circumstances, sandbags[11] might be required to protect property against rising and threatening flood waters. Although not a guaranteed measure against flooding, they can be quite useful in some situations as a barrier against oncoming water headed toward a property. Consider purchasing a supply of sandbags as a defensive measure against limited flood threats (if local hardware stores or lumber yards do not carry them, know which government agencies are responsible for distributing them, and under what particular circumstances). Sandbag barriers should supplemented with plastic tarp as an added seal against leaks in the barrier

  Also consider purchasing a *sump pump*. A sump pump is a device used for removing accumulated water from a particular location. Usually installed in the lowest level of a dwelling (such as a basement, where flooding often occurs), sump pumps operate by pumping excess water out of a home or building, and into nearby storm drains, ditches, or other water drainage channel. These machines can alleviate the extra expense of hiring private companies to drain water from a home or building, as well as limit the amount of potential water damage to property overall.

To help easily transport the items making up the flood disaster emergency kit, the items should be stored as a single unit. The best way to accomplish this is to store the kit in a container that is easily assessable in the event of need. Many hardware and discount retail stores stock plastic totes and bins of wide-ranging designs and sizes. Such containers can easily hold the items needed in the event of evacuation.

If all pre-flood precautions for high-risk areas are taken, the responsibility then shifts from preparation to simply being vigilant to potential flood situations. For each level of potential flood risk, there is an accompanying level of actions which should be taken with each flood threat situation. These levels of awareness are as follows:

During A Flash Flood/Flood Watch

Individuals should be aware of their risks for being affected by a flood, regardless of where they live and/or work. Particularly, people should be aware of the probability for flooding for their particular area. In all likelihood, those living in moderate to high-risk flood zones area are already aware of their

---

[11] When using sandbags, filling them is best accomplished at or near the site where they will be placed (i.e., used). Tying the open end of sandbags is generally considered a waste of valuable time and effort since doing so does not limit a collection of sandbags' effectiveness as a barrier. Among the most commonly used type of bags are untreated burlap sacks available at feed or hardware stores. Empty bags can be stored for emergency use, and will be serviceable for several years, if properly stored. Commercially purchased plastic sandbags, made from polypropylene, are available from most bag suppliers and store readily easily for an extended period of time. Sand can be purchased from any outdoor supply, landscaping, or gardening store. If needed in larger amounts, there are many local sand and gravel companies where sand can be purchased. See appendix for instructions and suggestions on erecting a sandbag barrier to protect property.

flood risks from either past experience, of by being informed by local agencies and/or real estate agents (who, in the U.S. are bound by law to reveal information about previous flooding).[12]

Local weather and/or news reports should be monitored for changes in conditions that might turn the potential for flooding from a possibility to an imminent certainty. A radio/weather radio, television, or internet news or weather feed should be accessible during this period in the event that an evacuation is ordered. Many news outlets now allow cell phone users to sign up to receive free text alerts on their phones in the event of weather or important news information. In addition, there are smart phone applications—many of them—available online that from various websites and "apps stores" that similarly keep smart phone users up-to-date on weather information. Having access to information regarding relevant news and weather updates allows those in a flood watch situation to know the various risks and hazards as they develop.

All modes of transportation (i.e., automobiles, vans, recreational vehicles) should be checked for adequate amounts of fuel. If fuel levels are questionable, it may be advisable to completely fill the tanks in the event that an evacuation order is given (or a quick escape becomes necessary; flash flooding can occur often with very little warning). Floods can and do often cause power disruptions, which includes powering the gas pumps at service stations. Should power become unavailable and vehicle fuel levels become critically low, the result could result in being stranded in an automobile while attempting to evacuate from an impending flood (and most flood deaths in the U.S. occur in automobiles).
Keep first aid supplies available, review flood safety plans, and be prepared to shut off utilities in the event of a flood warning and/or an evacuation.

During A Flash Flood/Flood Warning

Whenever a flood or flash flood warning is issued, and depending on the severity of the particular situation, this is the point in time when prearranged flood contingency plans should go into effect. In some cases flood threats may be less than either catastrophic or major, sometimes opting for simply monitoring local waterway levels or pumping small amounts of water from basements. In other circumstances, potential flooding can be so severe and dangerous that mandatory evacuations may be issued by officials.

If a flood warning is issued but no evacuation is warranted, *flood disaster emergency kits* should be gathered and kept nearby. Children and pets should be kept indoors or nearby as well, and away from rising waters, storm drains, viaducts, and/or sewers. Fuel levels in potential evacuation vehicles should be checked for ample amounts of fuel. Also, floods can directly impact one area with flood waters while affecting other areas nearby indirectly. For example, floods waters can overwhelm sewage treatment or water purification plants, resulting in possible contamination of water supplies. Under such circumstances, a *water-boil order* might be issued by local authorities.[13] Weather and news reports should be monitored, with a battery-powered radio or other news-assessable device nearby.

If flooding is of the slow-moving type (and not expected to rise to major or catastrophic levels), consider protecting property against encroaching waters by erecting temporary levees in the form of

---

[12] See appendix for resources on ascertaining flood risks for a given area across the United States.

[13] A water boil advisory/order is a public health advisory issued by local government or health agency authorities to communities when a community's drinking water is, or could be, contaminated by dangerous disease-causing contaminants. Boil orders are most common during flood-related situations or construction around water pipes.

sandbag barriers to reduce flood water damage. Sandbag barriers, properly filled and stacked can divert moving water around threatened property. And although sandbagging does not guarantee a water-tight seal, it is useful in many situations to delay or even keep water from flooding dwellings. Another step to take to limit flood damage for lesser-degree flood threats is to cover foundational openings into the home with plastic tarp or some other type of waterproof. Covering basement windows, crawlspaces, or other potential access points for flood waters into the lower levels of a home might provide an added –if not limited—level of protection against property damage.

However, if a flood warning is issued and the threat is severe enough where sandbagging is likely not to be effective in mitigating the potential damage to property, steps should be taken to leave the affected area as soon as possible (remember, it does not have to be raining for a flash flood to occur. This suggestion is also advisable for flood warnings with evacuation orders, even without a visible flood threat. Some of the most dangerous floods can have an origin point located many miles/kilometers away from where their waters can effect damage in populated areas). Water, electricity, and gas utilities should be shut off manually and all doors and windows should be closed and locked before leaving **if a flood is imminent**.

If driving away from affected and/or potentially affected areas, never drive through flood waters— even if they appear to be shallow (most deaths from floods in the U.S. occur in automobiles). The *flood disaster emergency kit* should be packed for transport. Automobile radios should be tuned in to a news station to hear updates on evacuation routes. The recommended evacuation routes should be followed, unless congested to the point of being a hazard themselves. If this is the case, consider an alternate route (keeping in mind that "shortcuts" or lesser known and isolated roads may already be blocked by flood waters). If leaving on foot, **do not** attempt to walk or drive through flood waters; seeking higher ground or contacting a friend or loved on outside of the affected area for a ride is the best course of action.

After The Flood

Generally, a flood threat is considered "passed" or ended when either flood waters begin to recede, when authorities indicate that it's safe to return to the affected area(s), or when meteorologists give the "all clear." Most of the period immediately after a flood can be expected to be spent cleaning up and repairing flood damage. However, during this time dangers still lurk in the affected areas, depending on the severity and duration of the flood.

Any building which continues to be surrounded by water should not be entered at all. A dwelling that was submerged in flood waters can still be potentially dangerous, particularly as a collapse hazard. If a building was flooded, it should be checked by qualified inspectors, building officials, or (if possible) emergency personnel for safety before anyone enters it. Such dwellings should be checked for structural damage, and their foundations for cracks or other damage. Other hazards to take note of include:

- Damaged gas lines, flooded electrical circuits, or submerged furnaces.
- The smell of gas or a "hissing" or blowing noise are usually indications of a gas leak; all windows should be opened and the building evacuated immediately should this situation be observed. In fact, all broken and/or damaged utility lines should be reported to the appropriate authorities.
- Electrical damage (sparks, broken or frayed wires, or the smell of burning insulation) should be noted if the utilities were not disconnected prior to evacuation. If power is still being supplied to the building, disconnect the electricity at the main circuit breaker—if it can be reached without stepping in any standing water.
- Damaged or water-logged walls, floors, doors, windows, and ceilings for risk of collapsing.
- Animals—domesticated or wild—which might have entered with the floodwaters.

Families returning to damaged homes after a flood emergency not only should observe the same potential post-flood hazards as those in other affected buildings, but should also expect to take actions to make their homes livable again. Most of these undertakings will involve eradicating potential immediate, intermediate, and long-term hazards caused by flood damage. Among the suggested courses of actions for those returning to flood-affected homes are:

- Flashlights are recommended to examine and search buildings, as opposed to combustion-based sources of light such as lanterns, torches or matches. Flammables may be inside. Under other conditions, these sources light are fine to use.
- Avoid visiting flooded areas. The presence sightseers and gawkers might hamper possible emergency operations.
- Any medicine, food, or water which has come into contact with floodwaters should be thrown out, including canned goods.
- Whether or not a boil-water order has been issued, it's a good idea to boil any water from a municipal source or well for 10 minutes or longer. Under such conditions, it's probably a better idea to purchase bottled water.
- Children and pets should be restricted from playing around flooded or dangerous enclosed areas where flood waters might remain.

- Windows and doors should be kept ventilation, and remaining flood waters should be pumped out of flooded basements gradually (removing about 1/3 of the water volume each day) to avoid structural damage.
- Electrical power should remain disconnected until an electrician has inspected the electrical system for safety issues. All electrical equipment should be checked and dried before being returned to service.
- Items composed of a large amount of fabrics such as bed mattresses and furniture should be thrown out, as they are usually unsalvageable. Other items that might have been exposed to flood water should be cleaned and disinfected.
- Seek necessary medical care. Even minor wounds or apparent illnesses.
- Contact the local Red Cross or other known charities to secure needed food, clothing, shelter, and first aid.
- Contact a service technician to check the function and electrical components of appliances left behind, otherwise consider disposing of nonfunctional items.
- Take pictures of property damage and make a record of lost or damage items for insurance purposes.

What to avoid

Just as there are measures to limit the potential for property damage and death from drowning and other dangers inherent in a flood threat, there are actions and decisions that one can make which may put one more in jeopardy, thus increasing risk the possibility of injury or even death. Fortunately, most possible negative consequences of bad decisions made during a flood emergency can be avoided by following common sense guidance. Actions to avoid during a flood include:

- Do not walk or drive through moving flood water. Because it's easy to underestimate the power and speed of moving flood water, most flood-related deaths in occurring in the U.S. every year are the result of people attempting to drive through moving flood waters (66% of flood deaths). Few individuals realize that it takes as little 6 inches (15 centimeters) of moving water to fell an adult human being; 2 feet (0.60 meters) of water can float a large vehicle even a bus. If floodwaters rise around an evacuation vehicle, the vehicle should be abandoned and higher ground sought if—if it can be done safely. If it becomes absolutely necessary to walk through water, wherever possible, walk where the water is not moving. A stick or other long instrument is advised as a means of checking the path for dangerous items under the water, hidden from view. Do not drive into flooded areas.

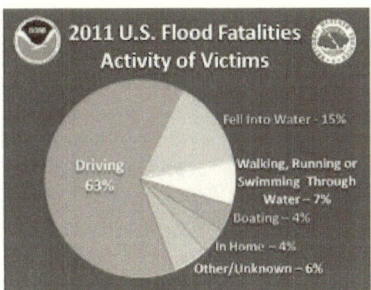

- Individuals should refrain from touching electrical equipment if it is wet, or if they are standing in water when attempting to do so.
- Do not drink water (unless it is bottled) unless it has been advised that it is safe to do so by local health or emergency management authorities. It is a good idea to continue using bottled water for a determined safe period after a flood (i.e., until such time when it there is an issued assurance that local tap water has been deemed safe for use).
- Avoid floodwaters; water may be contaminated by oil, gasoline, or raw sewage. Water may also be electrically charged from underground or downed power lines.
- Do not ignore the dangers of previously flooded areas. Roadways and paved surfaces may have been weakened by long-term submersion under water, and could collapse under the weight of a car or even an adult human being. One-third of flooded roads and bridges are so damaged by water that any vehicle trying to cross stands only a 50% chance of making it to the other side.
- Stay away from downed power lines, and report them to the power company.
- Do not enter homes or other dwellings unless a trained as a first-responder or assisting rescue personnel. Enter homes or other buildings only when authorities indicate it is safe. In addition, dwellings which are still surrounded by flood waters should be avoided as well.
- Do not avoid the necessity of servicing (or checking) damaged septic tanks, cesspools, pits, and leaching systems as soon as possible. Damaged sewage systems are serious potential health and environmental hazards.
- Do not overlook the need to clean and disinfect items that might have been covered with mud or that have been underwater. Mud left from floodwater may contain sewage and chemicals.
- Do not ignore orders to evacuate. If told to do so, leave as soon as possible.
- Do not underestimate the potential danger of a flood watch or warning. Weather advisories are issued in order to keep the public aware of threats and dangers to both property and life, and should be heeded. Remain vigilant under such circumstances.

Summary

Floods are one of the few natural disasters that man has—if only marginally—been able to make some efforts to control. And despite the advent and construction of flood-control measures such as dams, floodgates, canals, and other engineering marvels designed to control excess water, floods remain both a constant occurrence and threat, resulting in billions of dollars in damage and an estimated 25,000 deaths globally each year. The best way to deal with a flood avoid is to simply be elsewhere. Flood-threatened homes and private properties should be evacuated when ordered to do so. Even beyond the risk of possible fatalities, floods can damage property, destroy crops, and even devastate entire towns and regions. The great Mississippi River Flood of 1993, concentrated in America's Midwest covered an area 500 miles (804 kilometers) long and 200 miles (321 kilometers) wide. During that particular event, more than 50,000 homes were damaged, and 12,000 miles (19,312) kilometers) of farmland were washed out. As a threat to both life and property, preparing for the possibility of a flood emergency ranks as high as any other, and should be taken with as much earnestness as other such natural disaster emergencies.

Points To Remember

- The best way to avoid the dangers of a flood is to avoid being in the affected area. Statistically, this is the best way to avoid becoming a statistic.
- The best way to deal with a flood threat is preparation, especially in moderate to high flood risk regions.
- Weather radios, weather-related computer and cell phone applications, and local internet weather-related sites (including local news sites) are a good way to stay informed if during threatening situations.
- **If (weather) conditions become threatening, and there is a lingering doubt that the current residence isn't suitably distant from a potential flood threat, occupants should enact flood emergency contingency plans and leave.** Head to a designated emergency shelter or the safety of prearranged acquaintance's home.
- Do not attempt to drive through moving flood waters. It is easy to underestimate the force of flood waters, which is statistically dangerous.
- Remember the needs of family pets. Ensure that pets can be evacuated and remain with families. If not, then provisions should be made to shelter them in the event of a flood emergency.
- Do not underestimate the possible dangers lurking after flood waters recede. There as just as many potential health and injury hazards present in a post-flood environment—especially in urban flooding—as there are in the flood itself.

Notes

Flood History

The following flood-related historical events illustrate the potential for death which these events can inflict on affected reasons.

Date	Location	Impact/Significance
July-November 1931	China (regions along the Yellow, Yangtze, and Huai Rivers)	Considered the deadliest natural disaster of the 20th century (and one of the deadliest on record), the 1931 China Floods killed (estimated) between 2-4 million people.
September 1887	China (Yellow River Region)	Occurring during one of the river's regular flood cycles, the Flood of 1887 resulted in an estimated 1 million deaths (but as many as a million more may have perished in the flood, but is disputed due to the lack of records from the time).
December 26, 2004	Indonesia, Sri Lanka, India, Thailand, Somalia, various islands in the region	An estimated half-million people (possibly more) were killed as a result of floods triggered by a tsunami generated by one of the most powerful (undersea) earthquakes ever recorded.
May 31, 1889	Areas of the state of Pennsylvania (U.S.), including the city of Johnstown.	The sudden failure of the South Fork Damn on the Little Conemaugh River (triggered by heavy torrential rains preceding the event) caused the deadliest flood in U.S. history. The resulting wall of water killed more than 2,200 people.

Flood Control Measures in the U.S.

Dams

The John Martin Dam and Reservoir on the Arkansas River in Bent County, Colorado. The dam was constructed by the U.S. Army Corps of Engineers to control flooding on land areas along the river.

Flood Channels

Los Angeles River flows through a concrete channel.

Floodgates

Flood gates are put in place across Decatur street in Grand Forks, North Dakota as the Red River rises to flood levels in March 2010.

Floodways

The Morganza Floodway on the Mississippi River in Louisiana is opened by the U.S. Army Corps of Engineers to minimize the risk of catastrophic flooding to the cities of Baton Rouge and New Orleans as a result of recent heavy rains. The excess water is released into the nearby into the Atchafalaya Basin.

Levees

An earthen levee located in Texas.

Seawalls

The Bay St. Louis Seawall in Louisiana.

Appendix A

Glossary of Flood-Related Terms

100-Year Flood (or "multi-year" flood) is a flood event that statistically has a 1 out of 100 (or 1%) chance of being equaled or exceeded on a specific waterway in any given year. A flood event of this magnitude is often used to determine if flood insurance is either advisable or required on a property.

Canal (sometimes called a "channel") a canal is an artificial excavated waterway constructed to facilitate the flow of water. Flood canals can be natural or man-made, and typically are constructed alongside of levees and/or dikes in order to build up their depth. Constructed channels can be plain earth, landscaped, or lined with concrete, stone, or any other hard surface to resist erosion.

Dam is a barrier constructed across a waterway to control the flow or raise the level of water, often used to control flooding.

Flash flooding is the accumulation of water over normally dry land areas resulting from heavy or excessive rainfall in a short period of time, generally less than 6 hours. Flash floods are usually characterized by raging torrents after heavy rains that rip through river beds, urban streets, or mountain canyons sweeping everything before them. They can occur within minutes or a few hours of excessive rainfall. They can also occur even if no rain has fallen, for instance after a levee or dam has failed, or after a sudden release of water by a debris or ice jam.

Flash flood warning means a flash flood is imminent or occurring; take immediate action to protect life and property. A Flash Flood Watch may also be issued whenever there exist a potential for a levee breach or a dam break to occur.

Flash flood watch means a flash flood is possible in the watch area, and that conditions are more favorable than usual for its occurrence.

Floodgates are adjustable gates used to control water flow in flood barriers, reservoir, river, stream, or levee systems.

Floodplains are land areas adjacent to waterways that are routinely be covered by floodwater during a flood.

Flood Stage is the point at which the water level in a stream begins to cause damage to structures.

Flood warning is a weather alert indicating that flooding is imminent or occurring. It is a call to take immediate action to protect life and property.

Flood watch A watch is an advisory that alerts the public to the potential for overland flooding. It is considered a recommendation for planning, preparation, and increased awareness for changing weather.

Floodway is a waterway channel that is a portion of an adjacent floodplain that is designed to conduct an increase of water levels caused by flooding.

Flood zones are geographic areas that are recognized (usually by official channels) and defined according to varying levels of flood risk.

Levee is a man-made structure that is designed to contain or divert the flow of water. Levees may be comprised of an earthen embankment, but may often reinforced with cement, gravel, cement, or other earthen material.

Overland flooding is water that covers normally dry the land areas usually after heavy rains. In many cases, overland flooding is the result of the overflow of water after a creek or stream has surpassed its banks, or when the ground becomes over-saturated from water (such as those from heavy rains) due to poor drainage (natural or man-made). It is characterized by a gradual rising of water levels.

Sea level is the level of the ocean's surface, used in reckoning the height of geographical features, chiefly land areas and associated elevations, in proportion to it as a standard.

Urban and Small Stream Flood Advisory is advisory alerts the public to flooding which is generally only an inconvenience (not life-threatening) to those living in the affected area. This advisory is issued when heavy rain will cause flooding of streets and low-lying places in urban areas. Also used if small rural or urban streams are expected to reach or exceed their banks. Some damage to homes or roads could occur.

U.S. Army Corp of Engineers (abbreviated USACE) is a government agency under the Department of Defense. It is a major Army command made up of some 36,500 civilian and military personnel who are responsible for, among other responsibilities: (1) planning, designing, building, and operating locks and dams: (2) overseeing civil engineering projects that include flood control, beach nourishment (sand replacement due to erosion), and dredging for waterway navigation; and (3) designing and constructing flood protection systems through various federal mandates.

Watershed is an area from which water drains into a lake, stream or other body of water. A watershed is also often referred to as a "basin," with the basin boundary defined by a high ridge or divide, and with a lake or river located at a lower level usually recognized as a point for excessive water drainage within the basin.

Appendix B

National Flood Insurance Program: Regional Offices (FEMA)

As an extensive government agency, the Federal Emergency Management Agency's (FEMA's) administrative resources (as well as contact information) have been somewhat decentralized. This is to say that, in order to expedite any assistance to local and state governments (and to limit the potential for bureaucratic confusion), FEMA was divided into regional offices that oversee regional "zones." These *Regional Operations Offices* serve as the arms of the central agency's headquarters (located in Washington D.C.) and through which all policy, managerial, resource and administrative actions effecting coordination between headquarters are initiated. In addition, FEMA oversees the management of federal allocated assets and indirectly provides both funding and administrative resources for the National Flood Insurance Program (NFIP) for those in high-risk flood zone regions.

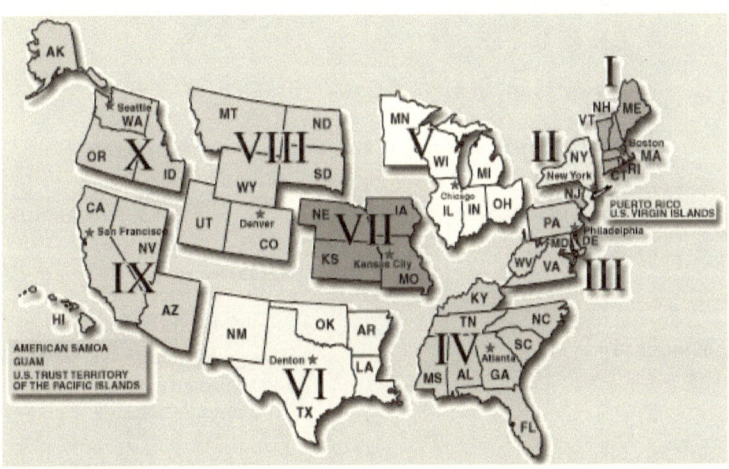

Region	Location	States Serving
Region I	Boston, MA	CT, MA, ME, NH, RI, VT
Region II	New York, NY	NJ, NY, PR, USVI
Region III	Philadelphia, PA	DC, DE, MD, PA, VA, WV
Region IV	Atlanta, GA	AL, FL, GA, KY, MS, NC, SC, TN

Region	Location	States Serving
Region V	Chicago, IL	IL, IN, MI, MN, OH, WI
Region VI	Denton, TX	AR, LA, NM, OK, TX
Region VII	Kansas City, MO	IA, KS, MO, NE
Region VIII	Denver, CO	CO, MT, ND, SD, UT, WY
Region IX	Oakland, CA	AZ, CA, HI, NV, GU, AS, CNMI, RMI, FM
Region X	Bothell, WA	AK, ID, OR, WA

FEMA National Flood Insurance Programs Regional Offices/Agents

LOCATION	NFIP AGENT REGIONAL OFFICE
Region I: (CT, MA, ME, NH, RI, VT)	**Thomas Young** P.O. Box 16321 Hooksett, NH 03106 Phone: 603-625-5125 Cell: 713-252-6779 Fax: 603-625-5125 TYoung@ostglobal.com
Region II: (NJ, NY, PR, VI)	**Walter McGuckin LUTCF** PO Box 7342 Penndel, PA 19047 W-267-560-5057 C-301-467-8103 F-267-560-5057 wmcguckin@ostglobal.com
Region III: (DC, DE, MD, PA, VA, WV)	**Walter McGuckin LUTCF** PO Box 7342 Penndel, PA 19047 W-267-560-5057 C-301-467-8103 F-267-560-5057 wmcguckin@ostglobal.com
Region IV:	**Lynne Magel ANFI** P.O. Box 1046

(AL, FL, GA, KY, MS, NC, SC, TN)	Zephyrhills, FL 33539-1046 W- 813-788-2624 C-813-404-8782 F- 813-788-2710 lmagel@ostglobal.com **David Clukie CFM (Region IV Liaison)** P. O. Box 10 Buford, GA 30515 W- 770-614-0865 C- 813-767-5355 dclukie@ostglobal.com
Region V: (IL, IN, MI, MN, OH, WI)	**Annette Burris CFM** PO Box 407 Petersburg, IL 62675 W-217-632-7210 F- 217-632-7210 aburris@ostglobal.com
Region VI: (AR, LA, NM, OK, TX)	**Carlton Watts** NFIP OK Office PO Box 13 Wewoka, OK 74884 W- 405-257-9000 F-405-257-9000 C- 301-928-3124 cwatts@ostglobal.com **Tom Kustelski (Region VI Liaison)** 929 Red Bluff Ranch Dr. Pipe Creek, TX 78063 Phone: 210-393-7857 Cell: 816-509-1949 tkustelski@ostglobal.com
Region VII: (IA, KS, MO, NE)	**Ally Bishop** PO Box 252 Louisburg, KS 66053 W-913-837-5220 C- 202-486-2738 F- 913-837-5220 abishop@ostglobal.com
Region VIII: (CO, MT, ND, SD, UT, WY)	**Erin May ANFI** 7125 West Jefferson Avenue Suite 400 **(Office at URS Building)** Lakewood, Colorado 80235 W-303-299-7873 C-303-550-3658 F-303-293-8585

	emay@ostglobal.com
Region IX: (AZ, CA, HI, NV, Guam, American Samoa, Mariana Islands, Marshall Islands, Micronesia, Palau)	**Adam Lizarraga ANFI** PO Box 492 West Sacramento CA 95691 F-916-375-0927 C-301-467-7291 alizarraga@ostglobal.com
Region X: (AK, ID, OR, WA)	**Kristin Minich CFM** 9300 50th Avenue NE Marysville, WA 98270 W-360-658-8188 C-830-265-7796 F-360-658-8188 kminich@ostglobal.com

Appendix C:
Disaster-Relief Organizations and Charities

This following is a partial list of the many disaster-relief and charitable organizations that those affected by tornado emergencies can turn to in times of need. Below is a sample of the most notable of these organizations.

American Red Cross
http://www.redcross.org/find-help

Catholic Charities USA
http://www.catholiccharitiesusa.org/what-we-do/disaster-operations/

Children's Disaster Services (Church of the Brethren)
http://www.brethren.org/cds/

Christian Disaster Response
http://cdresponse.org/

Feeding America
http://feedingamerica.org/need-help.aspx?s_src=Y14YPDGAA&s_keyword=feedingamerica&s_subsrc=feedingamerica

National Organization for Victim Assistance (NOVA)
http://www.trynova.org/

Salvation Army
http://www.salvationarmyusa.org/

Jewish federations of North America
http://www.jewishfederations.org/

World Vision

The No-Nonsense Guide To Flood Safety

http://www.worldvision.org/m/sponsor-a-child/?open&campaign=1193512&cmp=KNC-1193512&gclid=CI-G67v8pboCFYSd4AodMhgAIA

Appendix D:
Constructing Sandbag Barriers

Directions for filling sandbags:

1. Sandbags should be constructed close to the area of usage. Attempting to transport filled bags of sand not only waste valuable time, but could be prohibitively troublesome due to their collective weight.

2. Bags should be folded over the top of the bag as opposed to tying them off with a piece of string or other binding material. Again, doing otherwise tends to wastes valuable time in building a barrier. The expected water flow (if any) should run along the long side of the bag. The bag's fold should be tucked under the body of the bag, and tapped firmly in place with a shovel or with feet. This "tucking under" gives the next row of bags a flat surface to build on.

3. In constructing a temporary sandbag levee/dam, consider a pyramid-shaped structure. This particular shape in considered the most sturdy and reliable as a physical barrier against water. The general rule of thumb is to construct the base of the sandbag wall three times the height of the wall (see diagram below).

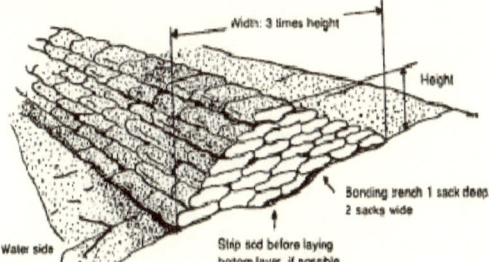

4. Because most sandbags are not waterproof, a plastic tarp or heavy waterproof sheeting should be used in conjunction with sandbags. Such plastic sheeting provides this type sandbag barrier its waterproofing. The sandbags themselves will provide enough weight to prevent the plastic from being washed or blown away. There may still be small leak along the barrier, but if the barrier is built effectively, the rate of any leakage will be minimal.

5. The sandbag levee/barrier should be placed/constructed around property facing the approaching water threat (e.g., such as a rising river).

Index

B

basin 11
    Mississippi River Basin 11, 12
      map of... 22

C

coastal flood watch 27
coastal flood warning 27

D

dams 5, 11, 21, 34 (picture)
    Aswan High Dam (Egypt) 21 (picture), 22
dikes (see: levees)

E

Emergency Flood Plan (development of...) 28-30

F

Federal Emergency Management Agency (FEMA) 15 (footnote), 28
    field/regional offices 44-47
flash flood watch 18, 31
flash flood warning 18, 25, 31, 32

floods 3 (defined)
    after floods (what to do after...) 33
    causes of... 4-5

References

"Defective Pumps Used to Protect New Orleans." 14 March 2007. *NBC News* website. Retrieved 19 August 2014

"Disaster Supplies Kit." *Disaster Center* website. Retrieved 10 August 2013

Edney, Ann, "Drowning Caused One-Third of Deaths from Hurricane Sandy." 23 May 2013 *Bloomberg.com* website. Retrieved 16 May 2011

Firestone, David. "We Built It: Flood-Control Edition." 29 August 2012 *New York Times* Website. Retrieved 19 August 2013

"Flood and Flash Flood" *Disaster Center* website. Retrieved 10 August 2013

"Flood Control Planning." *City Government of Mankato* website." Retrieved 10 August 2013

"Flood and Flash Flood." Talking About Disaster: Guide for Standard Messages. National Disaster Education Coalition: American Red Cross, FEMA, IAEM, IBHS, NFPA, NWS, USDA/ CSREES, and USGS pp 63-72.

"Flood Preparations." The Disaster Handbook 1998 National Edition Institute of Food and Agricultural Sciences University of Florida Publication DH-905 University of Florida Cooperative Extension Service (1998).

"Flood Warning Terms / Technical Terms." *Floodsafety*.com website. Retrieved 20 May 2013

Higgins, Andrew. "Lessons for U.S. From a Flood-Prone Land" NYTimes Page A6 (15 November 2012). Print

Julien, P. Y. River Mechanics. Cambridge University Press, UK. (2002).

Kaye, Ken. "Inland Flooding Causes Most Hurricane Deaths." South Florida Sun-Sentinel 16 May 2011. Print.

Kimmelman, Michael. "Going With the Flow" 13 February 2013. New York Times, Page AR 1. Print.

McDonald, Zack. "City Officials Unsure Why Flood Pumps Shut Down." 23 July 2013. *The News-Herald* website. Retrieved 30 July 2013

"Resources: Flood facts." *FloodSmart.gov* website. Retrieved 06 April 2013

Roberson, J.A., Cassidy, J.J., Chaudhry, M.H. Hydraulic Engineering, 2nd Edition, Wiley Press, USA. (1998).

Schwartz, John. "Vast Defenses Now Shielding New Orleans." 15 June 2012 New York Times. Page A28 Print.

"Severe Weather 101: Flood Basics." *NOAA National Severe Storms Laboratory Website*. Retrieved 06 April 2013

"So, You Live Behind A Levee." American Society Civil Engineers booklet (2010). Print.

"Stay Above Water: Flood Safety 101" 02 July 2013 *Weatherbug*.com website Retrieved 15 August 2013

"The Mississippi River and Its Floodplain." 04 March 2011. *The Nature Conservancy* website. Retrieved 10 August 2013

Turgut, Adnan and Tevfik Turgut. "Floods and Drowning Incidents by Floods." World Applied Sciences Journal 16 (8): 1158-1162 (2012)

US Army Corps of Engineers. After Action Report: May 2010 Flood Event Cumberland River Basin. (2002)
http://www.lrn.usace.army.mil/LRN_pdf/AAR_May_2010_Flood_Cumberland_Draft_V7_21.pdf

The No-Nonsense Guide To Flood Safety

The No-Nonsense Guide To Flood Safety

The No-Nonsense Guide To Flood Safety

http://www.mvd.usace.army.mil/About/MississippiRiverCommission(MRC).aspx

Page 13:
http://www.democraticunderground.com/10021668601

Page 20:
New York Observer
http://observer.com/2012/10/new-new-amsterdam-should-new-york-do-like-the-dutch-and-building-some-skyscraper-sized-sea-gates/

http://www.bangkokpost.com/learning/learning-from-news/258877/villagers-battle-irrigation-officials

Page 21:
City of Mankato website
http://www.mankato-mn.gov/Flood-Control/Page.aspx

Encyclopedia Britannica online
http://www.britannica.com/EBchecked/media/154698/The-Aswan-High-Dam-Aswan-Egypt

Page 23:

http://www.floodsmart.gov/floodsmart/pages/flooding_flood_risks/levees.jsp?cid=Fact_Sheet_FloodRisksLeveesForConsumers_012013_leveerisk

http://www.peacemakersinstitute.com/institute/?p=1533

Page 24:
Wikimedia
http://commons.wikimedia.org/wiki/File:Katrina_NOLA_levee_break_FEMA.jpg

Page 27:
http://www.dailymail.co.uk/news/article-1055660/After-storm-Floating-coffins-prowling-alligators-amid-Hurricane-Ikes-7bn-trail-destruction.html

Page 33:
http://publicsafety.ohio.gov/NPM/ReadyForEvacuation.stm

Page 35:
http://www.weather.gov/cle/2013_Flood_Safety_Week_2

The No-Nonsense Guide To Flood Safety

Page 39:
United States Army Corp of Engineers
Wikimedia
http://commons.wikimedia.org/wiki/File:USACE_John_Martin_Dam_Arkansas_River.jpg

Page 40:
USAToday.com
Wikimedia
http://commons.wikimedia.org/wiki/File:Opening_the_Morganza_Floodway_14_May_2011.jpg

Page 41:
http://blog.gulflive.com/mississippi-press-news/2011/08/katrinas_wake_corps_of_enginee.html

The No-Nonsense Guide To Flood Safety

Other Books in the No-Nonsense Safety Guide Series

Published By Lulu Books & Beyond The Spectrum

The No-Nonsense Guide To Tornado Safety

• Paperback: 84 pages • Publisher: lulu.com (November 22, 2013) • Language: English • ISBN-10: 1304648648 • ISBN-13: 978-1304648648 • Product Dimensions: 9 x 6 x 0.2 inches • Shipping Weight: 6.4 ounce

The No-Nonsense Guide To Blizzard Safety

• Paperback: 54 pages • Publisher: lulu.com (December 21, 2013) • Language: English • ISBN-10: 9781304709394 • Product Dimensions: 9 x 6 x 0.2 inches • Shipping Weight: 0.28 pounds

The No-Nonsense Guide To Flood Safety

The No-Nonsense Guide To Flood Safety.

• Paperback: 60 pages • Publisher: lulu.com (November 22, 2013) • Language: English • ISBN-10: 1304648613 • Product Dimensions: 9 x 6 x 0.2 inches

The No-Nonsense Guide To Hurricane Safety.

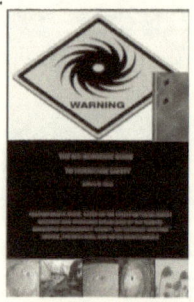

• Paperback: 59 pages • Publisher: lulu.com (December 20, 2013) • Language: English • ISBN-10: 9781304733030 • Product Dimensions: 9 x 6 x 0.2 inches

Other upcoming books in the series include: "The No-Nonsense Guide to Fire Safety," The No-Nonsense Guide To Earthquake Safety," and "The No-Nonsense Guide To Automobile Safety."

The No-Nonsense Guide To Flood Safety